Sorrows Refuge

Jessica Railsback

BookLeaf Publishing

India | USA | UK

Made with ❤ on the BookLeaf Publishing Platform
www.bookleafpub.in
www.bookleafpub.com

Dedication

To my heavenly hero. Though many do not believe in my God, His existence has been the life inside of my bones. Thank you for being my comfort throughout the sorrows of this life. You have been my inspiration in life and in writing.

Preface

Trials wean us from this world and prompt us to look to the happiness of the next world. -Thomas Baston Every human on this earth will suffer in some way or form at one point or another. This book was written to comfort the broken souls; pointing to the savior who comforts and restores the brokenhearted. This poetry collection is full of stories that one may suffer. Just as well there is a glimmer of hope resting and waiting to be found in each poem. Let these poems be a testament to the weaning from this world and the greatest hope of the next.

Acknowledgements

I want to make a special acknowledgment to my husband who encouraged me to do this project in the first place. He was my sounding board for almost every poem I wrote, giving me his honest opinion and constant support. Along with my oldest sister Samantha who gave me her expert opinion on the topics I knew less about. They both have been vital to the process of this book, and I'm extremely thankful.

1. Sorrows Refuge

Every heart is full of sorrows.
Unique to the battles they've endured.
Some are as vast as an ocean, some only shallow.
Leaving many broken or injured,
But there is no sorrow that can't be healed.
None too small or too great for a king.
Through whom all life was breathed.
He knows the aches within your grappling.
There is no requirement for refuge.
Only that one must choose.
Choose between life and subterfuge.
Some see suffering through a required bruise.
As if pain doesn't reach that level, it is void.
But Christ came to seek and save the lost.
One can be just as lost, without being destroyed.
To some, a penny is a pricy cost.
Their sorrows are not overlooked.
Just as the mighty sea is not too much,
For Christ to turn into a brook.
There is comfort in knowing His touch.

There is peace in surrender.
Just as there is healing for sorrow,
There is hope in a reminder.
There is no place that is too dark of a shadow.
That a light can't illuminate its past.
For Christ, there is nothing broken He can't heal.
His power is all too vast,
For Earth to win what it steals.

2. Chronic

The constant feeling of falling but never reaching the
end.
In pain but you cover it up with the way you pretend.
Everything is great, everything is fine, I'm doing just
alright.
Everything hurts, always on meds, just trying to fight.
One day may be good, but tomorrow could be another
hospital run.
So on those good days, you soak up every minute in the
sun.
Chronic illness makes you feel weak and lazy.
Longing to keep up standards and not feel hazy.
Felt obligation from the ridicule you heard as a kid.
What can we say? We didn't know better than what we
did.
The nails are chipped and your hair is falling out.
Your skin aches and burns, so you know it's another
bout.
Slept all day but your tiredness seems to increase.
The dragged-on days of feeling sick never seem to cease.

Each symptom is filled with sorrow that is a broken
reminder.
My body seems on course to kill me, or at least hinder.
As much as you would love to hang with your friends.
The continual restraint of ability is something you
resent.
Missing big events because you suddenly fall sick.
Or because you are avoiding the probability of being
pricked.
Feeling like a burden to others because you can't give
much.
Doing your best to stay healthy but you can't keep down
lunch.
Clinging to chairs, walls, or maybe your husband's arm
Just to avoid the possibility of bringing yourself harm.
The constant wondering if you have the strength to
make it through.
While hiding symptoms while at parties with the meds
that are new.
Sitting with a bible in the palm of your hands.
Trying your best to trust in the almighty's plan.
While wondering if it's a test, curse or not meant to be
understood.
Reminding yourself that all things work out for the good.
Whether it is here or on the other side of heaven.
Some things aren't meant to be a lesson.

Chronically ill is neither a punishment nor a curse,
But is a result of the original sins curse.

3. Church Pews

Church pews are hard and so became my heart.
Does my heart disregard those painful parts?
When I kneel before the cross.
I tremble for what I lost.
Hope differed makes the heart sick,
And the church walls thick.
Can I walk through those open doors?
And love those who are yours?
Those church pews are hard,
For those whose hearts are marred.
My faith should not be in a church.
For it causes a constant search.
Instead, my faith is in the one who loved.
Who's forgiveness is paid in the blood.
I'm called to obey despite what they do.
To still sit down on those hard church pews.
To love like Christ loved
To not be their judge.
Because It's not about me or the church.

It's about a God who heals the hurt.
At times I feel cornered.
But this is the only way to move forward.
To dress myself in self-control.
One of the many gifts that sealed my soul.
To walk through those open doors,
And love those who are yours.

4. Baby Blues

Searching for answers for something I wish was now.
Hope against hope that I could be pregnant somehow.
Researching symptoms that may be an existence,
But negatives have me choked up on a sentence.
Trying to find a balance of faith and reality.
Swinging too far spells the word calamity.
Disappointment kept silent amongst smiling faces.
Rejoicing in everyone's new phases.
Supplements fill up on a nightstand.
Heavily tracking ovulation and making plans.
Praising God because you know he is good.
The enduring ach when you don't think you could.
It is a lonely place to be.
When trying for a baby.
With its pendulum swings from high to low.
And the well meaning comments when no one knows.
Even if you trust God's Plan doesn't mean there's no ach.
Empty wombs cry out for the heart that breaks.
Pleading prayers for a miracle.
Relating to Hanna and repeating the cycle.

In full confidence you believe it will happen this time.
The hope in the failed attempt feels like a crime.
It is truly lonely in the two week wait.
When hoping to be in a motherly state.

5. Details

What is presumed as my weakness,
Is the exact recipe for my greatness.
It might be a fault for a doctor.
It will not make me look like a strong protector,
But it is a unique gift for my purpose.
Intended for a great service.
To think God created me with this in mind.
What I thought was a fault was God being kind.
Like a heroic story of destiny.
Is written in God's creativity of humanity.
Overflowing with a divine hope.
Once you discover the reason for the rope.
It is like a plot twist in a story.
Consuming the reader with God's glory.
It is a weakness that reveals a greater strength.
It is a purpose that gives life its length.
Instilled in us while being knit together.
The maker's forethought is truly clever.
Just an empty vessel being filled.
Reveals the tapestry God used to build.

The epic tale of how God will prevail.
And how he did it through every detail.

6. Battle of Virtue

Life is composed of evil and virtue.
Not all the things that bring happiness to you.
Happiness is not what brings life to a soul.
It is the heroic tale of good and evil that gives us a role.
We need something to fight against during the night.
And we need something to fight for during the light.
Many feel empty when they've achieved perfection.
Many wonder how they fell prey to that deception.
Happiness doesn't truly make someone happy.
Often they're confused as to why they feel sappy.
Life is like a good tale of old.
We need a heroic story to grab hold.
Take on a villainous battle or two.
Find a mission of virtue to do.
In doing so, you ignite a fire.
In doing so, you find yourself with a great desire.

7. Little Hand In Heaven

Can I hold your little hand in heaven,
After all this grief I'm left in?
I'm sorry I couldn't protect you until the very end.
All these emotions are so hard to comprehend.
I wish someone would have told me how lonely this is.
What I wouldn't do, to give you a thousand kisses.
A conversation hung between my husband and I.
Anxiety and fear ate me up inside.
Until shere disappointment came flowing red.
Once again, sickly lying with a hot water bottle in bed.
Did I do something wrong?
While crying, I listen to another sad song.
To lose something so precious as this.
It is the painful ach of falling into an abyss.
Maybe my home will never hear the patter of feet.
Maybe the ultrasound will show a heartbeat.
I get myself hopeful, just to fall into despair.
Not sure if it's worth coming up for air.
This is truly lonely indeed.
If only I could grow my little seed.

8. A Heart At Rest

Hold my hand, I'll squeeze it when I'm in pain.

Knowing you were there took away the strain.

All I ever wanted was to have you in my sight.

Then there you were dressed in white.

If only we could have had more time.

I would relish how your smile would always shine.

I hate to think it will dim when I'm gone.

I hope your heart will find peace to move on.

Just as mine does knowing you are here.

It makes me sad to know you are left with all this fear.

If I could, I would take it all away.

If I could, this wouldn't be my last day.

But it is.

So I leave you with this.

After today my heart will be at rest.

And all I ask is that you live your best.

I want you to be as happy as you have made me.

Since I can't stay, will you live a life for me?

Fill it with love, family, and the sweetest of dreams.

For I can't begin to express what all of this means.
You have given me the world in such a short time.
I only pray that one day, you will be fine.
My heart is at rest,
It's up to you to do the rest.

9. Beacon of Comfort

There is a comfort only God can give.
Giving the courage to continue to live.
Hope to continue the walk of a stumbling heart
A place to go when you don't know where to start.
It is an anchor in the tossing tides.
A refuge for the heart needing to hide.
Grounding the chaos inside your brain.
A shelter during the pouring rain.
God is a beacon drawing me home.
After getting lost by stumbling over a stone.
He calls me softly on the waters of peace.
My troubled heart knows where the pain will cease.
Run to the author of Forever.
Stilling the lip that quivers.
He is a place to go when you are left all alone.
Refreshing water for the plant that hasn't grown.
Many run to oblivion in a cup.
Oblivion of lovers, drugs, and living it up.
Yet it is all temporary.
None of it will make it past the cemetery.

Non reach the depths of a broken soul.
They only take what they already stole.
When my downcast heart is in distress.
There is only one place where a soul finds rest.
The feet that run to it know,
In times of need, there is no better place to go.

10. Imposter

Am I the imposter? Did I commit sabotage?
Because how I see myself seems like a moorage.
Tell me I'm great but I won't believe you.
Tell me I'm strong, but that ain't the truth.
I'm not lazy, I just doubt my ability.
So I won't follow through on my creativity.
I could succeed but I will feel like I failed.
With that, my focus will become derailed.
It's not what I expected and it's not what I hoped.
Feelings of embarrassment have me choked.
I can work for hours and have nothing to show.
Because the imposter inside won't let go.
Maybe I'm foolish, Maybe naive.
Maybe they will hate what they perceive.
My pen may be heavy and my ideas are full.
But perfectionism tells me they are dull.
Faults hang like guillotine over my head.
Unmet expectations filled with dread.
I know I should ignore these thoughts.
But somehow my mind gets caught.

I know these are lies that are holding me back.
But for some odd reason, I can't get back on track.
Half-finished projects sitting next to my big break.
Yet for some reason my mind can't see past the ache.
At one point we have to silence the imposter.
Let's put together our own roster.
One by one write down the truth.
One by one, remove the ache from your tooth.
Remember that ninety-two percent are lies.
That may be where this fear lies.
Remember you were given a purpose.
Find a way to bring it all to the surface.
Maybe then, the imposter will finally leave.
And then the magic can finally be conceived.

11. The Way It Ought

Who is this that I have met?
She is weighed down by regret.
I don't think she would like how she turned out.
She would disagree with all my doubts.
The girl painted in the past can't see.
The present picture of all that I believe.
Time moves on and creates a story picture.
It doesn't always look like the lecture.
Though the old me may not agree with me.
Time may influence how things are perceived.
I sometimes wonder what she must think of me.
Will she be disappointed in what I turned out to be?
But the hard truth is, she doesn't get a vote.
I can't keep carrying the past in a big old tote.
She is but a stranger kept by nostalgia.
Masqueraded as a guest in the gala.
Sometimes we have to say goodbye.
And finally decided to get off the ride.
The old has passed away and the new has come.
Realize change means that it will someday be gone.

Isn't that what we wanted to take place?
To be refined and renewed by grace?
It might not look the way she thought.
But maybe it turns out the way it ought.

12. Mockery

Do not mock my God.
This is the only time I don't spare the rod.
You can call me a Jesus freak,
But I won't stop my journey to seek.
Don't ask why a perfect God would make imperfection.
The gospel tells us good was corrupted when sin entered
creation.
That's why I share with you the good news.
If Christ didn't come we wouldn't be renewed.
Don't deny my God's authority.
Everything in this life is God's property.
When He returns, He will wipe imperfections from the
face,
Sparing only those who chose to be of faith;
Cleansing the evil that was left within.
Imperfection is the word believers call sin.
Judgment is a real thing we will all face.
The love believers talk about is His grace.
Don't mock the spirit that led me to belief.
Disgracing my savior causes immense grief.

I can not listen to the mockery of someone so precious.
He is so holy that my knowledge of Him has me
breathless.
I could lose everything I hold dear on this Earth.
Yet none of it holds such great worth,
Then the Lord of my heart who all creation sings.
Knowing there is truly no other greater king.
I can not allow one to vainly disgrace,
The Lord, who has my heart completely in His embrace.

13. Authentic

Do not say that at one time you were truly you.
As if you're running around normally confused.
You are always who you are no matter the change.
One's character is designed to act like a range.
There may be a base you naturally hold.
When life is not horrible or made of gold.
But in each moment it is you.
Whether controlled by fear or truth.
We will always have a side that comes out,
Depending on the circumstances that are about.
When life is good we will be more outgoing.
No doubt we like ourselves when we are glowing.
When life is tough we are likely to be reserved.
We often blame our timidity on what we observe.
It is folly to spend your life searching for your real self.
It would be like looking for a book, not on the shelf.
Our existence is not a journey to find who we are.
Our journey is so much greater than being the brightest
star.
Do you feel that deep-seated emptiness inside?

That's because we've hopped on the wrong ride.
We were supposed to get to know Jesus Christ,
But searching for self-identity is from the Antichrist.
Read the Psalms and see what they have to say about
faithfulness.
Listen to how the poet's suffering doesn't deter their
cheerfulness.
Get lost in the character of God's authority in the Old
Testament.
It enriches the instructions that you read in the New
Testament.
Salvation is going to bring the authenticity you were
looking for.
Seeking Him has more life than what you originally had
in store.

14. Suicidal

Once upon a time, I sat in a dark room;
Struggling to swim in the midst of gloom.
The pain I felt was growing more than my will to live.
Hope and optimism had not much left to give.
What kept the knife from my skin would be my God's
grief;
Fighting the desire to be in my God's relief.
Choosing obedience to my God until I was free.
Reminding myself that it was temporary grief.
My hands gripped the bible tightly.
Hungering the words of my Almighty.
Knowing weeping will only last a night.
But the joy comes with the morning light.
I held on as God fought my battles.
He fought for my heart that was fragile.
He held me in his arms as I cried in bed.
He was my comfort when all I felt was dread.
Little glimmers of light kept me alive.
Until freedom would finally arrive.
Some might spend forever on the pain they had;

But I share my grief because I see something glad.
I see the God who held my hand.
I see good despite evil man.
I see my God as my hero.
When my pulse was almost zero.
Some may only see pain when they look at evil;
But I see the heroic tale of God versus the Devil.
I see the joy and peace at the end of a good story.
More than all this, I see the amazing power of his glory.

15. Softer Sings

Still breeze and softer sings.
The little birdy telling me.
Not one sparrow, not one sorrow.
Is not seen by thy heavenly king.
For all that we know,
God has faithfully shown.
That he clothes the flowers,
In their desperate hours.
That his justices pursues,
The weight of truth.
Whether today I find relief
or I am kept in my grief.
I trust the hands that made me.
That he guides me to safety.
Whether on earth or in heaven.
Whether in joy or oppression.
Softer sings my soul,
For I trust the king in control.

16. Earthly Hero

I can't begin to explain, what it's like to have an earthly
hero.
Someone whose love makes you feel like you are not a
zero.
There is a feeling when you watch them protect you.
Evoking the deep thought of "Can this be true?"
Fireworks explode and an angelic glow surrounds.
The body is at ease when my hero is around.
Like a little kid, my eyes sparkle at his gaze.
He makes my heart still after being ablaze.
There is no word for this kind of love.
Only that it mimics the kind from above.
I don't know what I would do without him.
The lights of continuing would surely dim.
Dear Lord, don't take my earthly hero away.
For I don't think I would have the strength to stay.
My earthly hero has given me a reason to fight the
demons.
His love has strengthened me enough that it is a
weapon.

My earthly hero reflects my savior so well.
He makes living on Earth less like hell.
I hide behind my earthly hero like a shield.
While admiring the great valor he wields.
Tender is the warm touch of his hands.
Yet tough enough to take a mighty stand.
No villain is a match for the love God sends.
Where love is, violence ends.

17. The Letter

Dear child, I have not caused suffering upon your head.
This pain is not a punishment for something you did or
said.
It is a result of the curse when Eve ate the apple.
That is why I will return again to finish this battle.
Jesus died on the cross to pay the price on your head.
When he rose he conquered the eternal deathbed.
I have offered you freedom through belief.
Heavenly restoration doesn't mean you will see earthly
relief.
Some will suffer and cause earthly growth.
But that may not be the reason you must endure what
you loathe.
Not all pain has an earthly answer to find.
But let the pain wean you from sin and spiritually
remind.
This place full of suffering is not your home.
Nor is it just a holding place to roam.
I have a purpose for my children.
My will for your life is not hidden.

Obey my commands until I return.
Make disciples far and wide before it burns.
Do not draw conclusions for your pain.
Do not worry or fall prey to the strain.
I will deal with the answers and reasons.
In time you will see what I did with each season.
You're responsible for your response to the situation.
Just as evil will be accounted for in its devastation.

18. An Earnest Prayer

Forgive them, Lord, for they know not what they do.
I forgive them Lord, I ask that you would do that too.
It scares me Lord, that they will be punished for what
they did.
I used to relish that one day they would pay for what
they hid.
Not anymore my Lord; I wish them to be free from sin.
I take responsibility for my response within.
It is true that believers are supposed to love our enemies,
But that doesn't mean we should give them approval
amenities.
Give us wisdom and discernment between the two.
Let our actions reflect the truth that you want us to do.
Reveal any faults in my heart.
Let my feet be willing to do my own part.
Work in them as you continue to work in me.
Forgive them, just as you have forgiven me.
Move their heart towards you, I pray.
Spare them Lord, don't let them be prey.
I grieve the sin they cause.

Back to their vomit, just like the dogs.
Have mercy upon their head.
Don't let it follow them to their bed.
Let my response be pleasing to you.
Let not my heart sin against you.
This is my earnest prayer.
Don't let this end in despair.

19. A Torn Heart

My heart is torn between absolute excitement and
sorrow.
I want to show support, but my pain makes me feel
shallow.
Lord, guide my feet and give me the strength to smile.
The mix of feelings seems to build pressure after a while.
Is this envy to desire a good thing and not have?
I know God has given me much, and for that I'm glad.
How do I address the conflicting feelings inside?
Emotions are a gauge, not our guide.
To my knees, I fall before my King.
I seek comfort for what I think I need.
The pleas ring from my mouth.
The words of the desperate fallout.
When life is far out of my control,
There is only one who can consul.
He is my refuge for my unmet desires.
My prayers are not full of things I require.
But the comfort of knowing God knows exactly,
The feelings inside my mind and their quality.

Search me oh Lord, and find my heart is held in yours.
See that my life is waiting in the palms of your shores.
Let my head nestle into your chest.
In your arms, I wait to find rest.
I trust you my God, and that is why I come.
I come with all my emotions and their some.
In the end, the peace lets me be who they need.
To love them and give them everything.

20. A Grieved Soul

My soul is grieved by sinful man.
The heart is desperately wicked, who can understand?
My soul cries out to the Lord in agreeance.
With the evil that causes my God grievance.
It breaks our hearts to see the depravity.
In the wide-outstretched lack of morality.
Still, He is patient for the soul's repentance;
Not wanting to give all a death sentence.
I now understand why Abel's blood cried out from the
ground.
The holy spirit grieved, will cry out with a great sound.
Watching the blind lead the blind,
While everyone says they are fine.
Though you know that's not the truth,
So you know it is up to you.
Feeling helpless to actually make a difference.
When the disorientated proceed with confidence.
Allow me to stand up for those who can't.
Don't let my heart have a self-righteous chant.
Let my words only speak the truth they need to hear.

Don't let me shy away because of fear.
Guide my actions to be fruitful.
My success feels doubtful.
But to let someone be led astray,
I don't think I could live with that dismay.

21. Ancient Words

Ancient words, ever true.
Changing me and changing you.
Sits deep inside my heart,
When the worship team plays that part.
I am reminded how great is thy faithfulness.
And it washes away the earthly numbness.
It makes me want to sing "How great thou art".
And all the hymns that tug on my heart.
Each is so rich and full to the very end.
To know that Jesus is my friend,
Whom all my sins and griefs he bears.
I can bring it to my God in prayer.
When "Amazing Grace" plays,
I become gratefully humble in praise.
Knowing He gave me that blessed assurance,
Is all I need for insurance.
Oh, what a foretaste to see His glory divine.
Dear Lord and Father of mankind.
Abide with me every hour,
for I know your grace foils the tempter's power.

The hymns remind me I need thee.
I sing the songs with a heavenly plea.
So solid are the truths the hymns tell.
My soul knows that it is well.
When seas like billows roll.
No ink can fill up the whole scroll,
Of the good that God has done.
The songs ring out in one.
His love is so divine I can't comprehend his glory.
Scripture says that He is three times holy.
The hymns are a praise that can't be withheld.
For in heaven I long to one day dwell.